NOTE TO PARENTS

Welcome to Kingfisher Readers! This program is designed to help young readers build skills, confidence, and a love of reading as they explore their favorite topics.

These tips can help you get more from the experience of reading books together. But remember, the most important thing is to make reading fun!

Tips to Warm Up Before Reading

- Ask your child to share what they already know about the topic.
- Preview the pages, pictures, sub-heads and captions, so your reader will have an idea what is coming.
- Share your questions. What are you both wondering about?

While Reading

- Stop and think at the end of each section. What was that about?
- Let the words make pictures in your minds. Share what you see.
- When you see a new word, talk it over. What does it mean?
- Do you have more questions? Wonder out loud!

After Reading

- Share the parts that were most interesting or surprising.
- Make connections to other books, similar topics, or experiences.
- Discuss what you'd like to know more about. Then find out!

With five distinct levels and a wealth of appealing topics, the Kingfisher Readers series provides children with an exciting way to learn to read and wonder about the world around them. Enjoy!

Ellie Costa, M.S. Ed.
Literacy Specialist, Bank Street School for Children, New York

KINGFISHER
READERS

level
5

Ancient Egyptians

Philip Steele

KINGFISHER
NEW YORK

KINGFISHER
LONDON & NEW YORK

Copyright © Kingfisher 2012
Published in the United States by Kingfisher,
175 Fifth Ave., New York, NY 10010
Kingfisher is an imprint of Macmillan Children's Books, London.
All rights reserved.

Distributed in the U.S. and Canada by Macmillan,
175 Fifth Ave., New York, NY 10010

Library of Congress Cataloging-in-Publication data
has been applied for.

Series editor: Thea Feldman
Literacy consultant: Ellie Costa, Bank St. College, New York

ISBN: 978-0-7534-6768-8 (HB)
ISBN: 978-0-7534-6769-5 (PB)

Kingfisher books are available for special promotions
and premiums. For details contact: Special Markets
Department, Macmillan, 175 Fifth Ave., New York, NY 10010.

For more information, please visit
www.kingfisherbooks.com

Printed in China
9 8 7 6 5 4 3 2 1
1TR/0811/WKT/UNTD/105MA

Picture credits
The Publisher would like to thank the following for permission to reproduce their material.
Every care has been taken to trace copyright holders. However, if there have been unintentional
omissions or failure to trace copyright holders, we apologize and will, if informed, endeavor
to make corrections in any future edition.
Top = t; Bottom = b; Center = c; Left = l; Right = r
Cover Shutterstock/Ian Stewart, Shutterstock/sculpies; Pages 5 Corbis/Robert Harding; 6 Corbis/
Fridmar Damm; 8 Corbis/Christine Osbourne; 11 Art Archive/Dagli Orti/Egyptian Museum, Cairo;
12 Shutterstock/sculpies; 13 Shutterstock/Ian Stewart; 16 Getty/De Agostini; 17 Shutterstock/RCH;
19 Margaret Maitland; 22 Art Archive/Dagli Orti; 23 Art Archive/Musée du Louvre/Dagli Orti; 27b
Shutterstock/Vladimir Wrangel; 28 Art Archive/Musée du Louvre/Dagli Orti; 34 Shutterstock/RCH;
35 Corbis/Aladin Abdel Naby/Reuters; 36cl Shutterstock/maeadv; 36b Corbis/Ben Curtis/epa;
37bl Corbis/Sandro Vannini; 37br Shutterstock/tamaguramo; 38 Werner Forman Archive/British
Museum; 39cr Art Archive/Egyptian Museum Cairo/Kharbine-Tapabor/Boistesselin; 40 Corbis/Roger
Wood; 41 Art Archive/Gianni Dagli Orti; 42 Art Archive/Egyptian Museum, Cairo/Dali Orti;
43 Corbis/Otto Lang; 44 AKG/Egyptian Museum, Cairo; 45 Corbis/Bettman.

Contents

Opening the tomb

In ancient Egypt, there was a secret valley. It was hidden among rocks and cliffs on the edge of the desert. It was a burial place for the **pharaohs**, the rulers of ancient Egypt. Today it is known as the Valley of the Kings.

In 1922, an **archaeologist** was looking for tombs in the valley. His name was Howard Carter. One day, he found a hidden door buried by stones and earth.

Tutankhamen's treasure had been buried for thousands of years.

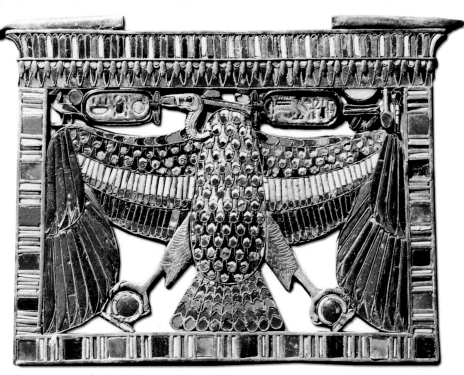

This fine jewelry was made of gold and colored glass.

Carter broke open the door and peered inside. He could see a gleam of gold. The tomb was filled with piles of treasure! It held jewelry, **ivory**, weapons, royal thrones, and statues. The tomb belonged to a pharaoh named Tutankhamen, who died in 1324 BCE. People all over the world were amazed by Howard Carter's discovery and the treasure of Tutankhamen.

Teenage king

Tutankhamen was not a very important king. He died when he was a teenager. Even so, his body was placed in a beautiful coffin made of gold.

The mighty Nile

If you fly over Egypt in a plane, you see large sandy deserts. The land is hot and dry, and only a narrow green strip marks the course of a big river, called the Nile.

Boats still sail up and down the Nile River today.

The Nile carries rainwater from central Africa all the way to the Mediterranean Sea. Before the river reaches the coast, it splits into many separate streams. This region of Egypt is called the Nile **delta**.

In ancient times, the river flooded every summer. The floods left behind thick black mud. This soil was very good for growing crops, which was why farmers first settled along the banks of the river thousands of years ago.

People used the river for watering their fields. It also gave them water to drink. They made boats from reeds or wood to travel up and down the river. Without the Nile, the ancient Egyptians could not have survived.

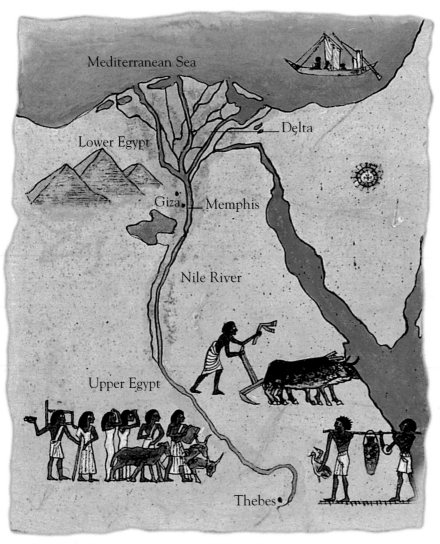

Mediterranean Sea

Delta

Lower Egypt

Giza Memphis

Nile River

Upper Egypt

Thebes

The Nile is about 4,145 miles (6,670 kilometers) long. It is the longest river in the world.

Gods and goddesses

The Egyptians believed in many different gods and goddesses. Some of them were a part of nature or were linked with wild animals or birds. Painters showed the gods in pictures with horns or beaks or the heads of animals.

Ra was the sun god. A god named Anubis was responsible for **mummies**. Osiris was the god of the dead, and his wife Isis was the mother goddess. Horus was the god who looked after Egypt and its pharaohs.

People believed that the eye of Horus had healing powers.

How many gods?

There were at least 740 Egyptian gods and goddesses. A pharaoh named Akhenaten believed that there was just one god, named Aton, the disk of the sun. His ideas did not last. His son, Tutankhamen, went back to worshiping all the old gods.

Ra   Osiris   Isis   Horus   Anubis

The Egyptians believed that the pharaohs belonged to the family of the gods. They also believed that if the pharaohs did not do their duty, the whole world could fall apart and there would be a state of **chaos**.

The kingdom of Egypt

The southern lands around the Nile were called Upper Egypt, and the northern lands were called Lower Egypt. More than 5,000 years ago, both regions became one country, ruled by a pharaoh.

Most pharaohs were men, but one woman, named Hatshepsut, did rule as pharaoh. Pharaohs wore crowns and headdresses and lived in grand palaces. The queen and royal family made up the **royal court**, along with the nobles. There were also many powerful officials, top priests, and army leaders.

Other important people were doctors, engineers, **architects**, craftworkers, and priests.

Snake and bird

The badge of Lower Egypt was the cobra, a deadly snake. The badge of Upper Egypt was a bird called a vulture, which eats dead animals. The two became **symbols** of royal power.

First comes the royal family. Then there are the top people, called nobles. They include leading priests, officials, and army commanders.

In the third row are doctors, engineers, traders, **scribes**, and architects.

The fourth row has minor priests and craftworkers.

In the fifth row are soldiers, sailors, servants, and performers.

At the bottom are laborers and slaves.

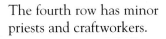
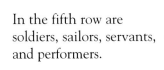

The big pyramids

Between June and September every year, the Nile flooded the fields. Laborers could not work on the land, so instead they had to help build temples or **monuments**.

Laborers built **pyramids** near the ancient city of Memphis on the orders of the pharaohs. These were like mountains made of stone blocks. One big pyramid, in a place called Saqqara, is more than 4,600 years old. It has four sides, with steps. A hundred years later, the Egyptians built three pyramids in Giza that were even bigger and had smooth sides.

The Giza pyramids are still standing today.

A strange monster

Near the pyramids of Giza there is a giant, mysterious statue. It has the body of a lion and the face of a king. It is called the Great **Sphinx**.

Pyramids marked the tombs of dead pharaohs. The Egyptians believed that the spirit of the pharaoh went to the world of the gods, where he would live forever. They filled the tombs with treasures that the pharaoh could use in the next world.

Building in Giza

The biggest monument in Giza is the Great Pyramid. It is the tomb of a pharaoh named Khufu.

Building the Great Pyramid probably took thousands of workers more than 20 years. It was made from more than 2.3 million stone blocks, each weighing between 2 and 15 tons. The stone was cut from quarries and carried down the Nile in barges. Then laborers loaded it onto wooden **sleds** and dragged them over rollers to the site.

The builders probably built **ramps** from mud brick and soil to pull the stones up. Later they knocked the ramps away. Secret tunnels led to the burial chamber, sealed with massive stones. Even so, their treasures were stolen by robbers.

Wonder of the world
The Great Pyramid was 482 feet (147 meters) tall, and it was the tallest building on Earth for thousands of years. Over time, the wind and sand have worn it down, and today it is 456 feet (139 meters) high.

Priests and temples

The ancient Egyptians built big stone temples. These had high gates as well as courtyards with tall pillars. In the center of each temple, there was a holy **shrine**, with statues of the gods.

A pharaoh makes an offering to the god Aton.

Priests or priestesses offered food or drink to the gods. They burned **incense** and played music. They had to stay very clean and pure. Priests shaved their heads and washed at certain times of the day in a sacred pool. They could not wear wool or leather or eat fish. Some special priests wore leopard-skin robes.

Ordinary people could not enter temples to worship the gods. Sometimes there were big religious festivals when the priests took the statues of the gods out of the temples. They carried them in processions or up and down the river in boats.

Perfect place

Karnak was the biggest and most important religious site, and the ancient Egyptians called it the Most Perfect Place. It was near the ancient city of Thebes, and it took 1,300 years to build. There were three main temples and a sacred lake.

Ways of writing

Egyptian priests invented a way of writing made up of pictures and shapes. The symbols stood for sounds, ideas, or things. We call these symbols **hieroglyphs**, which means sacred carvings. Hieroglyphs were carved on temples and monuments for thousands of years.

The Egyptians also invented other ways of writing. These flowing scripts were quicker to use. People used black or red ink and pens made from reeds. Officials who could write were called scribes.

The Egyptians made a type of paper from **papyrus**. Papyrus was a tall reed that grew by the river. The stalks were stripped, soaked, and pressed together.

Hieroglyphic writing uses pictures of things such as animals, plants, food, objects, and buildings to make words and sentences.

People sometimes wrote quick notes or practiced their handwriting on broken pottery.

After ancient Egyptian times, people forgot how to read the old writing. Then, in 1799, some soldiers found a piece of stone in a place called Rosetta. It showed Egyptian scripts written next to ancient Greek words, which people still understood. About 20 years later, people had figured out how to read hieroglyphs. This helped us understand ancient Egypt.

Living in towns

The Egyptians built villages, towns, and big cities such as Memphis and Thebes. Cities had walls to protect them from attack.

City streets were made of hard earth. Bricks made from mud mixed with pebbles and straw were dried in the sun until they were hard. Even royal palaces were made of mud brick and then covered in painted tiles.

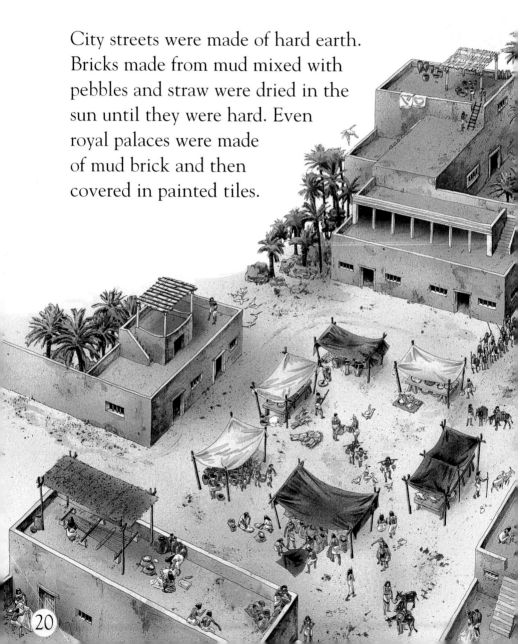

During the day, the streets were noisy. Markets were held in open squares between the houses. There were donkeys, children, and the hammering of metalworkers, jewelers, and furniture makers. Craftworkers made pots, leather sandals, and baskets.

Some Egyptian houses had two or three floors, with beams made from palm tree trunks. People sat or slept on the flat roofs in the cool of the evening.

Going to the bathroom
Egyptian toilet seats were often made of wood. They stood above a pottery jar filled with sand.

The farmer's year

Most Egyptians lived in villages in the delta or along the riverbanks. Farmers dug channels to bring water from the river through their fields. They also grew crops at **oases**, which were the few places in the desert where there was water.

Every November, oxen pulled plows over the soil. Farmers scattered seeds by hand. Herds of sheep or goats walked over them to push them into the ground.

A farmer plows his land. Dates are growing on the palm trees.

Women made bread from the grain grown and harvested by farmers.

Villagers used **sickles** made of wood and stone to harvest the wheat and barley. They made bread or beer from the grain. They grew vegetables such as peas, beans, cabbages, leeks, and cucumbers. Dates, figs, grapes, and melons were sweet and healthy food crops. When there was a poor crop, people went hungry.

Farmers kept ducks, geese, pigs, goats, and cattle to eat, and they raised sheep for their wool.

Hippo havoc!

In some areas, hippopotamuses came out of the river at night and made a mess of the crops on the banks.

23

Food and feasts

Egyptian workers were paid with food instead of money. They stored food in pottery jars and cooked in a clay oven. At a simple meal, they might eat onions, beans, salted fish, or fruit. The bread must have been a little gritty because the teeth of ancient Egyptians were often worn down.

Nobles enjoyed hunting. Sometimes they brought home wild ducks from the river or a deer from the desert, to serve at a feast. Beef stews or roast goose might be on the pharaoh's table, along with vegetables cooked in milk and cheese, tender figs, **pomegranates**, and delicious honey cakes. The Egyptians drank red and white wine.

The nobles of the royal court loved grand **banquets**. They wore their finest clothes and jewelry. During and after the meal, the guests watched musicians, acrobats, and dancers putting on a show.

Sweet pastries
Cakes and rolls came in all shapes and sizes. Some were like doughnuts, while others were shaped as triangles or spirals. Some bakers made cakes in the shape of crocodiles.

Fashion and beauty

How do you keep cool in a hot country? The Egyptians wore light, loose clothes made of plain white linen. Women wore a long dress with shoulder straps. Men wore a tunic or just a **kilt**, a length of cloth worn around the waist like a skirt. Their clothes were sometimes decorated with pleats or folds.

Most people in the royal court wore clothes made of white linen.

Laborers and servants wore **loincloths**. Poor people made sandals from papyrus or grass, while rich people wore leather sandals. Children often ran around naked.

Nobles wore beautiful jewelry and broad collars made of beads. Both men and women wore makeup. The Egyptians made black eyeliner from a type of lead and lipstick from **ocher**, a red earth. They loved perfumes and scented oils.

Boys had shaved heads and a side lock of hair. Many men shaved their heads too, and both men and women often wore wigs.

Nefertiti was a powerful and beautiful queen. Look at her headdress, collar, and makeup.

27

Everyday life

Children played with rattles, balls, spinning tops, and toy lions and crocodiles. They wrestled and swam.

Most children had to work. Boys helped in the fields or learned skills in their father's workshop. Girls learned how to weave cloth and cook.

Children from important families, especially boys, learned reading, writing, and math. They were beaten if they made mistakes.

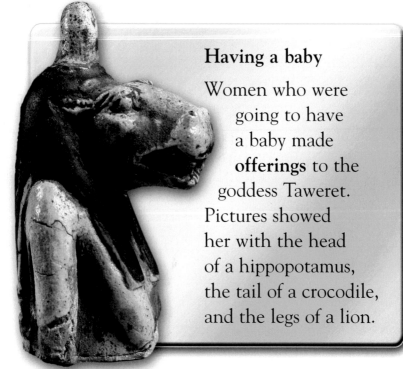

Having a baby

Women who were going to have a baby made **offerings** to the goddess Taweret. Pictures showed her with the head of a hippopotamus, the tail of a crocodile, and the legs of a lion.

Women married before the age of 15, and men married by the time they were 20. Marriages were arranged by the parents, although love did play a part in choosing a husband or wife.

Poor people often died by the time they were 30 or 40, but rich people could live to be 70 or older. One pharaoh, Rameses II, was about 90 when he died.

Making mummies

Egyptians believed that after they died, they would be with the gods forever. They wanted their bodies to be turned into mummies. This made sure that the bodies kept their shape and could travel safely to the world of the gods.

To make a mummy, the priests first cleaned the body. Then they pulled the brain out through the nose using a hook. They cut out the guts, liver, lungs, and stomach and then dried them and put them in jars.

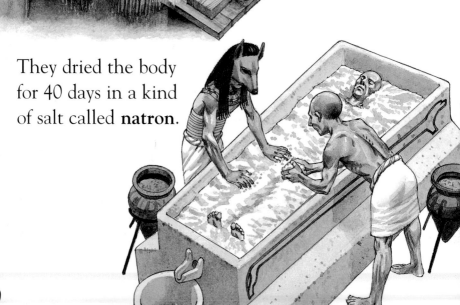

They dried the body for 40 days in a kind of salt called **natron**.

Then they stuffed the body with linen cloth or sawdust. It was covered in gum and oil and wrapped in linen bandages, with lucky charms. They put a mask over the head.

Ancient mummies are still being discovered today. Archaeologists study them carefully. They can find out from mummies what people ate and how they lived and worked.

Sacred kitty

Egyptians also made mummies of cats. They buried them to honor the cat goddess, who was named Bastet.

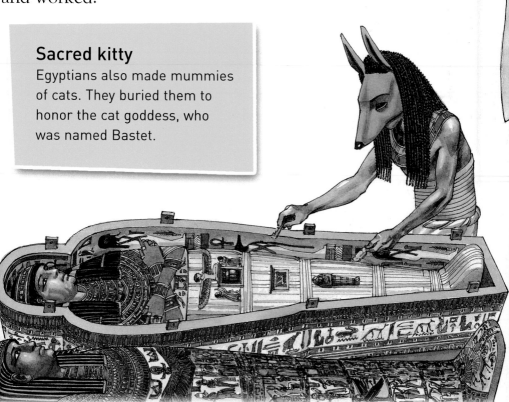

A funeral procession

The mummy makers placed the body inside a wooden coffin in the shape of a human body. They painted the wood to look like the person who had died.

Royal mummies might have several coffin cases, one inside the other. A large stone chest called a **sarcophagus** held the coffins in the tomb.

At the royal funeral procession, long lines of women wept and wailed. Priests made offerings to the gods, sprinkling milk and burning sweet incense. The coffin was hauled to the burial ground by oxen on a sled shaped like a boat.

In this boat, the dead pharaoh traveled to meet the god Osiris, who ruled the world of the dead.

Priests carried out one last **ceremony** to make sure that the pharaoh could come back to life in the next world. They called this Opening the Mouth. Then they placed the body in its tomb.

A dead pharaoh is taken to his tomb.

Food for the dead
There were stone tables near the entrance to the tomb. People left food and drink there to feed the mummy's spirit.

Raiders and robbers

Pharaohs stopped marking their tombs with pyramids and began hiding them underground because robbers kept breaking in to steal the treasure.

At first, the Valley of the Kings seemed like the perfect place for royal burials. It was hidden in cliffs on the edge of the desert west of Thebes and could be easily guarded.

The Valley of the Kings was used between about 3,500 and 3,000 years ago.

Great discoveries are still being made in Egypt.

The tombs were full of dead ends and deadly drops to keep the robbers from reaching the royal treasure. Robbers broke into many tombs anyway.

Archaeologists have found 63 tombs or burial places in the Valley of the Kings. Nearby there is also a Valley of the Queens and a Valley of the Nobles. Wall paintings in many of them tell us about life in ancient Egypt, but most of the treasure disappeared thousands of years ago.

Death to robbers!
Anyone who robbed a pharaoh's tomb faced a terrible punishment. They could be stuck on a pointed wooden stake!

Treasures of Tutankhamen

The most famous tomb ever found in Egypt belonged to the young pharaoh Tutankhamen. His tomb was smaller than others, but because robbers had not taken away all the treasures, it was packed with beautiful things. Archaeologists think that robbers did try to break into the tomb but may have been disturbed.

Howard Carter, the man who discovered the tomb, spent years working on it, clearing passages and chambers and making lists of all the wonderful things he found. There were chariot wheels and trumpets, daggers, bows and arrows, painted chests, and golden thrones.

A beautiful ring found in Tutankhamen's tomb and his golden mask

How did he die?

Tutankhamen's remains have been scanned and x-rayed several times in recent years. Some archaeologists claim that the young king was murdered. Others believe that he had an accident, hitting his head and breaking his leg. Some think that he died of a fever after the accident.

Tutankhamen is taken away for an x-ray.

Carved wooden animals, cups, beds, and stools lay beside board games, jewels, fans, and golden sandals. There were even boxes of food for the pharaoh to eat on his journey to the world of the dead.

In 1925, Howard Carter opened the inner coffin and gazed at last on the mummy of Tutankhamen. Over the face was a mask of solid gold and a blue stone called **lapis lazuli**.

Traders and explorers

The Egyptians did not use money or metal coins in the time of the pharaohs. They exchanged goods or services. This way of swapping things is called **barter**. At the market, they swapped grain for pots and jars, or jewelry for a knife.

At the market, the Egyptians used scales to weigh goods for bartering.

The Egyptians sometimes used rings of copper, silver, or gold in their exchanges. They might swap a bed worth 20 units of copper for a wooden chest of the same value.

The pharaohs exchanged precious gifts with the rulers of other countries. The Egyptians built sailing ships and traded with other peoples who lived around the Mediterranean Sea and Arabia. Egyptian explorers sailed down the Red Sea to a land they called Punt. This was probably somewhere in East Africa. They brought back ivory, precious woods, incense, and wild animals such as pet monkeys and sacred baboons.

Long-distance trade

Traders brought the valuable blue gemstone known as lapis lazuli all the way from Afghanistan to Egypt— about 2,500 miles (4,000 kilometers).

Bracelet with lapis lazuli

Egyptian ships arrive in Punt.

Egypt at war

The Egyptians believed that their pharaohs
should rule all the lands created by the gods.
Pictures show the pharaohs crushing Egypt's
enemies. Egyptian soldiers fought against Nubia,
the African country to the south. Their armies
marched west into Libya and east into Asia.
The pharaoh Rameses II fought a great battle
at Qadesh against a people called the Hittites.

An Egyptian army goes to war. These
models were found in an ancient tomb.

Rameses II
in his chariot
at the Battle
of Qadesh

The Egyptians built strong forts from mud bricks.
Soldiers were called up to take part in battles or
expeditions, and slaves could win their freedom by
fighting in the army. They fought with bows and arrows,
swords, axes, and spears and carried shields and clubs
called **maces**. They hurled stones at the
enemy with **slings**. The first metal weapons
were copper. Later weapons were made of
bronze and iron.

Egyptian armies
began to use chariots
pulled by horses about
3,500 years ago.
Archers stood on
them to fire arrows
at the enemy.

Victory!

In 1456 BCE, a pharaoh
named Thutmose III
fought a battle for the
city of Megiddo. The
Egyptians captured
2,000 horses and
924 chariots.

After the pharaohs

In the end, the Egyptian pharaohs lost their power over Egypt. Other peoples came to rule the lands around the Nile River, including the Persians, Greeks, Romans, Arabs, and Turks.

New cities were built. The port of Alexandria became a great center of learning. Cairo became the biggest city in Africa, but the world forgot the old ways of life in Egypt. Sand covered the ruined monuments. During the 1700s and 1800s, Europeans became interested in ancient Egypt. They carried away monuments and treasures to their own countries.

Then archaeologists began to work in a more scientific way. They took more care of ancient temples and tombs and built a new museum in Cairo.

The mayor of Thebes with his wife and daughter

Moving a temple

In the 1960s, the Egyptians built a new **dam** in
Aswan, which raised the water level of the Nile
River. The Great Temple of Abu Simbel had to
be taken apart and moved to higher ground,
where it was rebuilt.

Today and forever

Egyptian archaeologists are still searching for ancient remains. In 2009, they found 30 mummies inside one tomb in Saqqara. They had been there for 2,600 years.

Today visitors come to Egypt from all over the world. They travel up the Nile River and explore the ancient pyramids, temples, and tombs. Tutankhamen is the most famous pharaoh still lying in the Valley of the Kings. He is more famous today than he was in his own lifetime.

A beautiful cup was found in Tutankhamen's tomb. On it was the following message:

May your spirit live on,
May you spend millions of years, you who love Thebes,
With your face to the wind from the north
And your eyes seeing happiness.

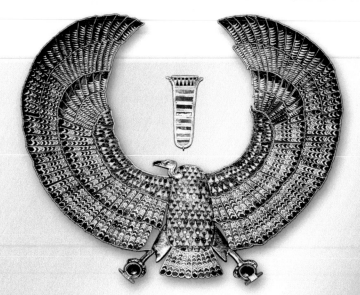

Ancient Egypt key dates

BCE

ca. 6000	Farmers grow crops around the Nile.
ca. 3400	Walled towns are built in Egypt.
ca. 3100	Egypt is ruled as one kingdom.
ca. 2650	The stepped pyramid is built in Saqqara.
ca. 2560	The Great Pyramid is built in Giza.
ca. 2500	The Great Sphinx is built in Giza.
ca. 1550	Burials take place in the Valley of the Kings, near Thebes.
1483	Queen Hatshepsut dies.
1478	The Battle of Megiddo ends with a victory for Thutmose III.
1379	The pharaoh Akhenaten brings in sun worship.
1324	The pharaoh Tutankhamen dies.
1274	The Battle of Qadesh is fought by Rameses II.
525	The Persians rule Egypt.

Glossary

archaeologist someone who studies ancient remains and ruins

architects people who design buildings

banquets feasts for many guests

barter to swap one thing for another instead of buying or selling it for money

BCE before the Common Era (any date before 1 CE). It is also sometimes known as BC.

ceremony a public action carried out by priests or officials

chaos complete disorder and confusion

dam a wall built across a river to control its flow

delta a coastal area where a buildup of mud forces a river to split into separate streams

hieroglyphs picture writing used in ancient Egypt

incense wood or gum that smells sweet when burned

ivory elephants' tusks

kilt a length of cloth worn around the waist like a skirt

lapis lazuli a blue gemstone

loincloths short pieces of cloth tied around the waist

maces club-like weapons

monuments large statues or pillars in public places

mummies dead bodies that have been dried and prepared so they do not rot

natron a type of salt

oases water holes in the desert where plants can grow

ocher a sort of earth colored red, brown, or yellow

offerings food, drink, or objects offered to a god or goddess

papyrus a type of paper made from reeds

pharaohs rulers of ancient Egypt

pomegranates a kind of fruit grown in warm countries

pyramids four-sided monuments that have a square base and triangular sides rising to a point

ramps slopes of soil or rock

royal court the people around a ruler, including the royal family, nobles, and officials

sarcophagus a stone chest made to hold a coffin

scribes people whose job is to copy writing or make notes; officials in ancient Egypt

shrine a holy place built to honor a god

sickles curved cutting blades used to harvest crops

sleds large wooden boards used for transporting heavy loads

slings straps used for hurling stones at an enemy

sphinx a statue with the body of a lion and the head of a human

symbols things that stand for other things

Index

If you have enjoyed reading this book, look out for more in the Kingfisher Readers series!

KINGFISHER READERS: LEVEL 1

Baby Animals
Butterflies
Colorful Coral Reefs
Jobs People Do
Snakes Alive!
Trains

KINGFISHER READERS: LEVEL 2

What Animals Eat
Your Body

KINGFISHER READERS: LEVEL 3

Dinosaur World
Volcanoes

KINGFISHER READERS: LEVEL 4

Pirates
Weather

KINGFISHER READERS: LEVEL 5

Ancient Egyptians
Rainforests

For a full list of Kingfisher Readers books, plus guidance for teachers and parents and activities and fun stuff for kids, go to the Kingfisher Readers website: **www.kingfisherreaders.com**